THE FIRST-TIME GRANDMOTHER'S JOURNAL

The FIRST-TIME Grandmother's Journal

Inspiring Prompts to Celebrate Your Experience with a New Grandchild

LISA CARPENTER

ILLUSTRATIONS BY MEL BAXTER

R

ROCKRIDGE
PRESS

For general information on our other products and services or to obtain technical support, please contact our Customer Care Department within the United States at (866) 744-2665, or outside the United States at (510) 253-0500.

Rockridge Press publishes its books in a variety of electronic and print formats. Some content that appears in print may not be available in electronic books, and vice versa.

Interior and Cover Designer: Brian Lewis
Art Producer: Hannah Dickerson
Editors: Andrea Leptinsky, Nicky Montalvo, and Samantha Holland
Production Editor: Emily Sheehan

Illustrations © 2020 Mel Baxter

Author photo courtesy of Jambl Photography

ISBN: Print 978-1-64739-885-9
R0

Contents

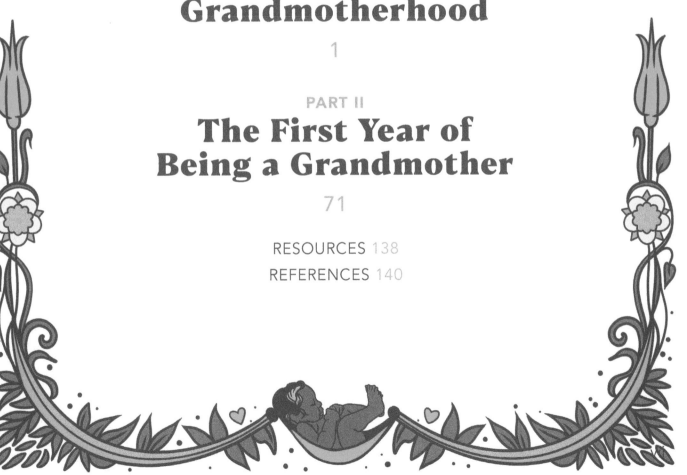

Introduction

Congratulations, dear grandmother-to-be, your grandmother journey has begun!

This journal will assist you in creating and chronicling that journey and your unique role. Thought-provoking prompts encourage first-time grandmothers to explore, appreciate, and record their thoughts, feelings, events, and experiences, from first hearing a grandbaby is on the way—whether that be via traditional childbirth, surrogacy, adoption, etc.—through the first year of that baby's life.

This journal is a keepsake for you. Just as the journey is solely yours, so is this record of it. Though you may one day choose to share with others, meaningful entries flow more freely when kept confidential.

There are two parts to this journal. The first will help you prepare for the initial stages of grandparenting, from the announcement that a baby is on the way to the birth. The second provides you with creative opportunities to preserve details on must-remember moments, from the first time holding the precious newborn through celebrating their first birthday.

Journal prompts in both parts—some simple, some a little more challenging—fall into seven categories, inspiring you as a new grandmother to reflect on significant aspects of nurturing yourself and your grandchild.

1. **Being Present:** How, when, and why living in the moment matters as a grandmother.

2. **Doing Your Part:** What kind of grandmother do you hope to be, and how will you realize that vision?

3. **Exploring Your Wisdom:** Life experiences and lessons shape us. Which ones are you compelled to pass along?

4. **Forming a Bond:** Recognizing that grandmother-grandchild connections run the gamut, from breezy to not so easy.

5. **Living in Love:** Revering, recording, and remembering the euphoric, boundless love of a grandmother.

6. **Looking Ahead:** Exploring hopes, ideas, and dreams for your grandchild, your child, and yourself.

7. **Looking Within:** Reflecting on and improving upon maternal matters past, present, and to come.

I have been where you are now, fellow grandmother. When my middle daughter and her husband announced their pregnancy in 2007, my second thought was, *Do I have what it takes to be a grandma?* My first thought? A heart-expanding hallelujah at the news.

But once the confetti settled and I acclimated myself to residency on cloud nine, I grappled with the grandmother job description. Must I learn new skills? Eradicate old habits? Become comfortable uttering "sweetie bug"?

I didn't fit the stereotypical grandma mold, and that concerned me. So I researched the position. I (subtly, secretly) studied grandmothers around me. I devoured books and articles written by and about grandmothers. My research revealed that the grandmother stereotype is a fabrication, a misrepresentation. Grandmothers cannot be pigeonholed. Every grandmother is a unique blend of intentions, interests, beliefs, behaviors, skills, and stories. The only commonality: They love their grandchildren.

Realizing that no grandmother fits the stereotype assured me that I did, indeed, have what it takes to be a grandma. I just needed to be true to myself and define the role on my own terms, in my own way.

I discovered much about myself that first year as I embraced my grandmother status. Soon after my first grandchild celebrated birthday No. 1, I started a grandma blog highlighting those lessons learned and the grandma lifestyle—my lifestyle—to negate that pesky grandmother stereotype. I've also profiled nearly 200 grandmothers on the site, exploring how every woman approaches the grandma gig on her own terms, in her own way.

In the more than 12 years since my life-changing, life-affirming first grandson arrived, the number of goofy, grand boys who call me Gramma has grown to four—plus two "bonus" step-grandsons who call me by my first name. At the time of writing, my eldest daughter is set to deliver her second child (another boy!), my final grandchild as my three daughters declare their families complete. Though the size of my family might have stopped growing, I won't. I'll continue defining—and redefining—my grandmother journey.

Grab a pen and prepare for fun as you define your unique journey! Your promotion to motherhood's next level deserves documenting in real time, for all time. Once complete, you can revisit this keepsake annually on your first grandchild's birthday, as a poignant reminder of who you were when your grandmother journey began—and how far you've come.

PART I

Preparing for Grandmotherhood

Welcome to the first stage of grandmotherhood, the life-changing point at which your title of *mother* transitions to forever include the word *grand*.

And grand indeed are the moments and months that make up this first stage, from the moment you learn the exciting news to witnessing the astounding growth of your grandchild—as well as the profound changes in the parents-to-be.

Becoming a grandmother brings profound changes for you, too, as the family you began years ago grows into a new generation. You may wonder how you will be present for your new grandchild or how you can best help your child in their new role as a parent. There's much to remember and record, and plenty to ponder and put into practice. Let's get started.

Living in Love

You're going to be a grandma! Where and how was the life-changing announcement made to you? With whom did you first share the news?

Looking Within

Learning your child will be a parent can stir up a surprising mix of emotions, all of which are valid. Circle the words that best describe your thoughts and feelings upon the announcement.

Anticipation	Joy
Anxiety	Nervousness
Calm	Relief
Concern	Resignation
Contentment	Sadness
Enthusiasm	Shock
Glee	Speechlessness
Gratitude	Stress
Happiness	Surprise
Impatience	

Expand on those feelings on the lines provided.

"When a child is born, so is a grandmother." – Jan Miller Girando

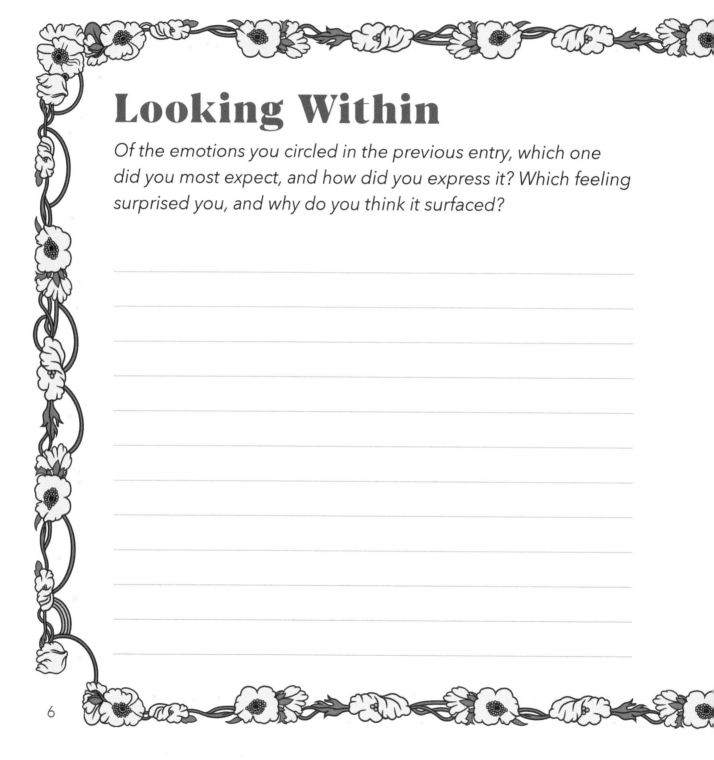

Looking Within

Of the emotions you circled in the previous entry, which one did you most expect, and how did you express it? Which feeling surprised you, and why do you think it surfaced?

Being Present

Relax. Let your chin fall to your chest. Close your eyes and take a deep breath in. Exhale. Consider all you are grateful for in this moment, and then record it here.

"The birth of a child heralds a precious time, one that has the power to transform all the adults touched by the experience into more loving people." – Jerry Witkovsky

Forming a Bond

In what ways is the relationship with your child, the grandchild's parent, changing as they approach parenthood? How do they accept guidance or advice from you, whether unsolicited or requested?

Being Present

Grandmothers tend to juggle fewer responsibilities than mothers, yet habits like multitasking and social media fixation can make it harder to live in the moment. What lifestyle changes might improve your mindfulness as a grandmother?

"Perfect love sometimes does not come until the first grandchild."
– Welsh proverb

Looking Within

Think back to when you first learned you'd be a mother. What challenges—emotional or otherwise—did you face? What about once your baby arrived? How are those challenges resurfacing now?

Looking Ahead

Based on your response in the previous entry, describe three self-improvement goals for yourself to overcome the residual fears and challenges of the past or that you now face as a grandmother.

1. _____

_____

_____

2. _____

_____

_____

3. _____

_____

_____

A Tip for Journaling

Concerned your writing skills aren't worthy of a keepsake? One key is to approach this journal as you would a diary that you may have kept years ago. This is *your* record for *your* eyes only. There's no pressure, no right or wrong answer, no "grandmother guru" to reprimand you for missing a mark.

Approach each prompt one by one without considering the whole. Read the prompt, and then contemplate your initial response. First thoughts and gut feelings typically speak truth; try to capture those without judgment. Big words and correct grammar don't matter—authentic entries straight from the heart do.

Doing Your Part

Some grandmothers take a hands-off approach to grandchildren, while others assume full responsibility. The participation level of most falls in between. Circle tasks you'll cover and cross out those you won't.

Assume full custody, if necessary

Babysit for short periods

Babysit overnight

Bathe

Change diapers

Expose to nature

Feed

Give gifts of toys, books, clothing, experiences

Love unconditionally

Pay for education

Pay for lessons, activities

Play with

Provide regular childcare

Provide treats

Read to

Relocate near grandchild

Rock, cuddle, snuggle, hug

Share your faith

Share your skills and hobbies

Take on vacation

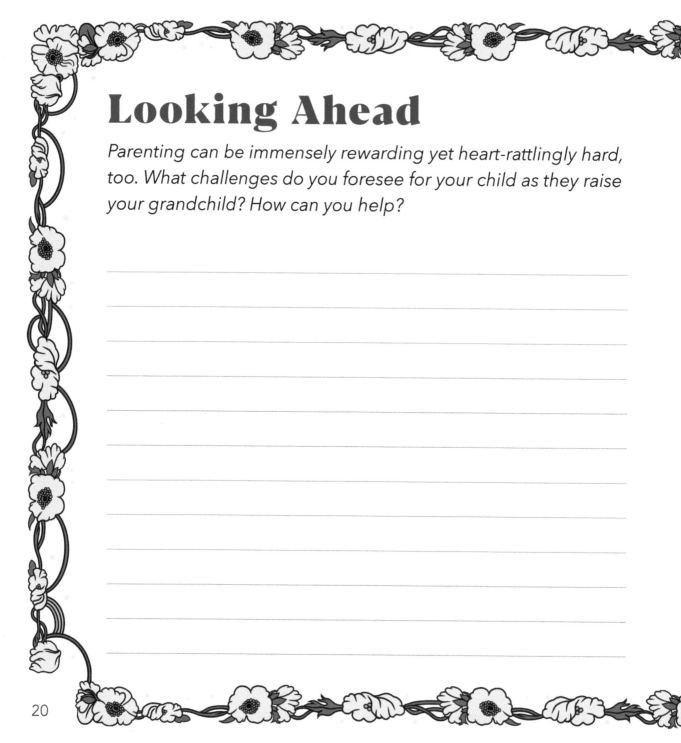

Looking Ahead

Parenting can be immensely rewarding yet heart-rattlingly hard, too. What challenges do you foresee for your child as they raise your grandchild? How can you help?

CAPTURE THE DETAILS!

Baby's Sonogram

Use this space to add a picture of your grandbaby's sonogram. If you don't have one, feel free to include any other pictures, like one of the proud parents-to-be.

TAPE
SONOGRAM
HERE!

Looking Ahead

Create a collage of what you hope your grandchild's future will look like and include. Use words and images you sketch, cut from magazines, or print from your computer.

Exploring Your Wisdom

Your decades as a mother earned you reams of experience.
What mothering tricks, tips, and techniques will be useful for you
as a grandmother?

"If becoming a grandmother was only a matter of choice, I should advise every one of you straightaway to become one. There is no fun for old people like it."
– Hannah Whitall Smith

Looking Ahead

What non-holiday rituals will you establish with your grandchild? A designated grandma–grandchild playdate? A special storybook to read together regularly? Starting and contributing to a keepsake collection? List your ideas below.

Exploring Your Wisdom

You are a unique grandma, yet you aren't your grandchild's only grandparent. That's great! Experiencing the influence of multiple adults enriches children. What skills, interests, and experiences exclusive to you will broaden your grandchild's view of the world?

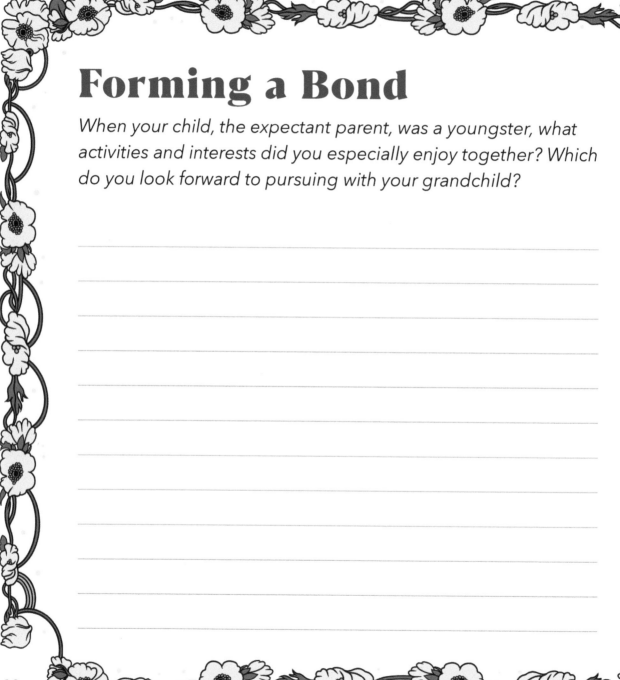

Forming a Bond

When your child, the expectant parent, was a youngster, what activities and interests did you especially enjoy together? Which do you look forward to pursuing with your grandchild?

_____

_____

_____

_____

_____

_____

_____

_____

_____

_____

_____

_____

_____

_____

_____

_____

"Grandmotherhood initiated me into a world of play, where all things became fresh, alive, and honest again through my grandchildren's eyes. Mostly, it retaught me love." – Sue Monk Kidd

Doing Your Part

Your grandchild's birth will be a defining moment for you. If you will become a grandmother by childbirth, do you you want to witness the delivery? Wait at the hospital? Await a phone call? If your grandchild will become part of your family in a different way, what are your wishes regarding their arrival? What are the parents' wishes?

How to Be Present

Mindfulness and *being present* are terms that sound ideal yet can seem utterly unachievable considering their intangible character. But once you grasp a few principles and the importance to your grandmother-grandchild relationship, being present can become second nature and your most effective tool as a grandma.

The act of being present is simple: Do one thing at a time. Stop multitasking. Clear your calendar, your mind, and your space, and focus on what's in front of you.

Mindfulness takes practice. Begin now and you'll be adept by grandbaby's arrival. Here's how:

- ◆ Consciously practice doing one thing at a time.

- ◆ Be intentional in focusing. Relax, take a deep breath, close your eyes, clear your mind, and then slowly exhale.

- ◆ Eliminate external distractions such as electronics, social media, and clutter.

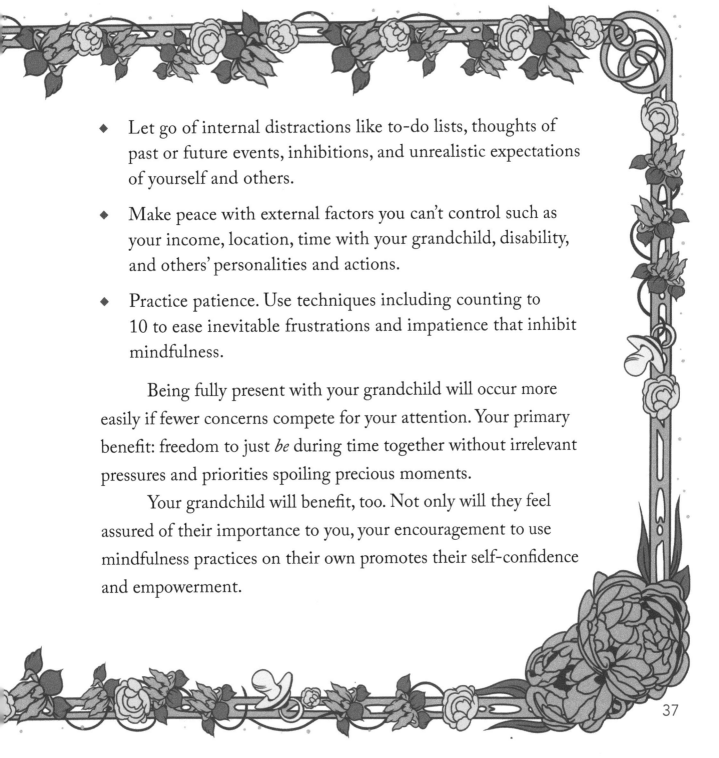

- Let go of internal distractions like to-do lists, thoughts of past or future events, inhibitions, and unrealistic expectations of yourself and others.

- Make peace with external factors you can't control such as your income, location, time with your grandchild, disability, and others' personalities and actions.

- Practice patience. Use techniques including counting to 10 to ease inevitable frustrations and impatience that inhibit mindfulness.

Being fully present with your grandchild will occur more easily if fewer concerns compete for your attention. Your primary benefit: freedom to just *be* during time together without irrelevant pressures and priorities spoiling precious moments.

Your grandchild will benefit, too. Not only will they feel assured of their importance to you, your encouragement to use mindfulness practices on their own promotes their self-confidence and empowerment.

Exploring Your Wisdom

What was your experience when your grandchild's parent arrived in your life? How is that experience reflected in conversations with your expectant child about your forthcoming grandchild?

Forming a Bond

Some grandmother-grandchild bonds happen effortlessly; others require more intention. Regardless of how or when yours forms, what will a healthy bond with your grandchild look like?

"With your own children, you love them immediately—and with grandchildren, it's exactly the same." – Kevin Whately

Doing Your Part

Grandmothers are so special and made of captivating qualities. Fill in the blanks with traits for your Ideal Grandmother recipe.

The Ideal Grandmother Recipe

A plentiful portion of _____

Equal parts _____ and _____

A heaped helping of _____

A sprinkling of _____

A pinch of _____

Generous dashes of _____

Combine well, then spread over grandchildren. Reapply without reservation.

In the space provided, express why these qualities are important to you.

Being Present

Dwelling on your parenting missteps or how the new parents may raise your grandchild might hinder your focus on the baby. What could you let go of in order to better appreciate every moment?

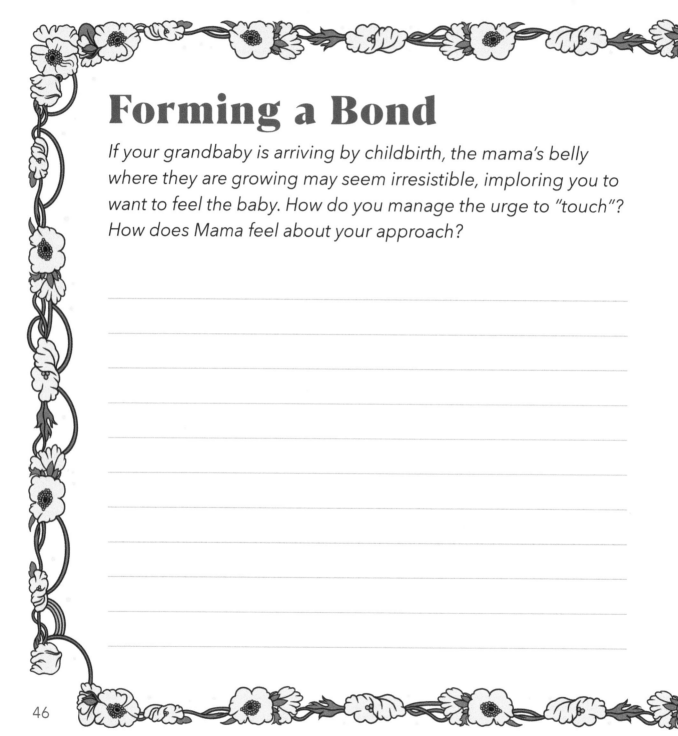

Forming a Bond

If your grandbaby is arriving by childbirth, the mama's belly where they are growing may seem irresistible, imploring you to want to feel the baby. How do you manage the urge to "touch"? How does Mama feel about your approach?

"You are a giver of kisses, a provider of treats, and a source of unconditional love and solace. You are a grandmother, and your grandchildren know exactly what to call you." – Honey Good

Exploring Your Wisdom

Mothers often give parenting advice out of love, but adult children may perceive it as Mom wanting control. Describe your degree of freedom or constraint when sharing wisdom with the expectant parents.

Being Present

Describing heightened emotions surrounding grandmotherhood can be hard. Colors help. Think "tickled pink" or "green with envy." With crayons or colored pencils, surround each phrase with color befitting your related feelings.

Becoming a grandmother

My grandchild's mother

My grandchild's father

My grandchild

The "other" grandma

My mother

My maternal grandmother

My paternal grandmother

My grandchild's future

In the space provided, explain why each color was chosen.

Doing Your Part

Smartphones filled with digital images are alternatives to grandma brag books packed with photos of cherished grandchildren. How will you save, share, and show off photos of your beloved babe? What fun ways have you found to preserve precious memories?

_____

_____

_____

_____

_____

_____

_____

_____

_____

_____

_____

_____

_____

_____

_____

"Truth be told, being a grandma is as close as we ever get to perfection."
– Bryna Nelson Paston

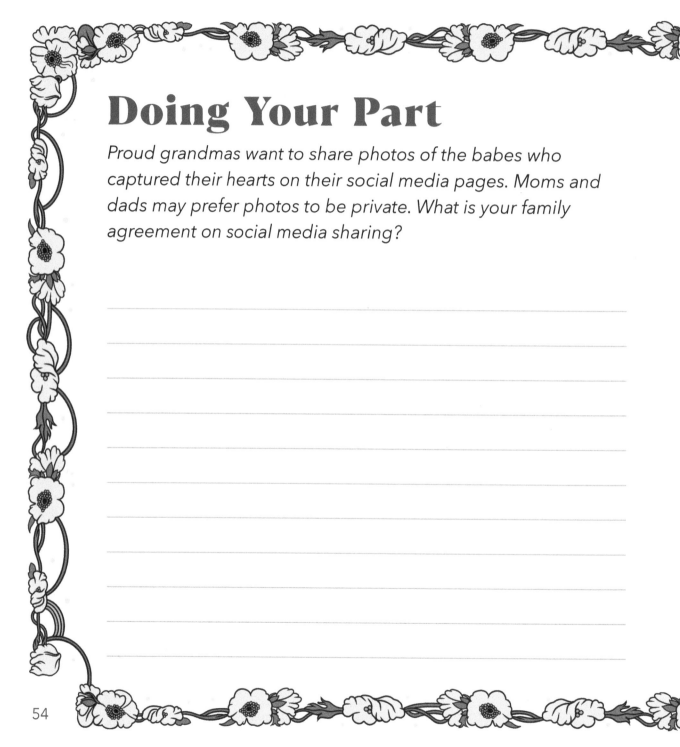

Doing Your Part

Proud grandmas want to share photos of the babes who captured their hearts on their social media pages. Moms and dads may prefer photos to be private. What is your family agreement on social media sharing?

What Tips Would You Share with Other First-Time Grandmothers?

Congratulations on surviving stage one of grandmotherhood! The anticipation, anxiety, excitement, delight, and amount of patience required can wring ragged even the most hip, happy, and healthy grandmother. Having successfully navigated to month nine, what tips have you developed so far that may benefit grandmothers whose journeys have just begun?

Living in Love

Grandmothers love to do things for their grandchildren. Beyond physical acts, what intangible things do you want your love to do for your grandchild? Support? Comfort? Educate? Encourage? Describe how.

Looking Within

Traits and behaviors often persist from generation to generation, whether physically passed down or learned. Which of yours do you see in your child? Which do you hope your grandchild inherits? Which do you hope they don't?

"Then, wham! My first grandchild was born . . . I was jolted, blindsided by a wallop of loving more intense than anything I could remember or had ever imagined."
– Lesley Stahl

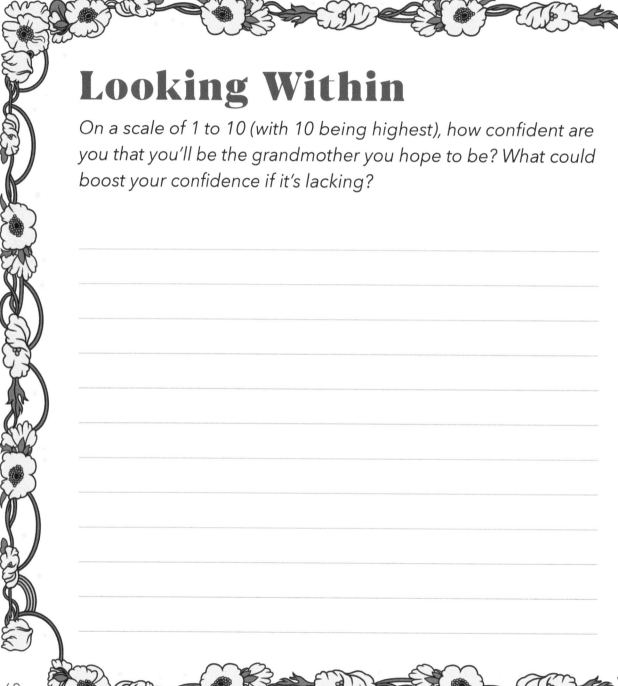

Looking Within

On a scale of 1 to 10 (with 10 being highest), how confident are you that you'll be the grandmother you hope to be? What could boost your confidence if it's lacking?

Living in Love

Compose a social media post or text message—short, sweet, 280 characters or less—to the parent of your grandchild describing what their gift of your first grandchild means to you. (Need more characters? Go long and start a thread!)

Looking Ahead

Your grandbaby arrives soon! Complete the acrostic poem using words and phrases that reflect what you hope to share with them in years to come.

G _____

R _____

A _____

N _____

D _____

C _____

H _____

I _____

L _____

D _____

CAPTURE THE DETAILS!

Who's on My Support Team?

List folks who will welcome your grandmother stories, fawn over your grandchild photos, and readily offer a hug, hand, an ear, or advice as needed.

Write a Letter

What wisdom will you share with your grandchild?

You have a lifetime of experience juggling hard knocks and happiness in measures you alone know. Contemplate the wisdom you gleaned from the good, bad, ugly, and otherwise along the way, and then compose a letter to your grandchild. Bestow upon them insights you gained before their arrival enriched your world.

PART II

The First Year of Being a Grandmother

Congratulations! That bitsy bundle you eagerly awaited has arrived, forever expanding your heart and broadening your world.

One simple act finally eases your months of anticipation: holding your precious grandchild in your arms for the first time.

The unforgettable first look and first snuggle with your sweet one mark the start of many memorable firsts: Grandbaby's first smile, first step, first reaching out to you, your first time babysitting, the moment you grasp the reality of your child being a parent, your first grandmother growing pains.

Your grandmother journey now hits high gear. Treasure this time and savor every step.

Living in Love

Oh, that glorious first glimpse of your grandchild! What was your first thought, first feeling, and first reaction upon seeing your grandbaby?

Being Present

Grandchildren are so deliciously delightful, you want to just gobble them up. It's best, though, to savor them with senses other than taste. Describe ways your grandbaby affects your senses.

Sight: _____

_____

Smell: _____

_____

Touch: _____

_____

Hearing: _____

_____

CAPTURE THE DETAILS!

Baby's Here!

Record details of your dear one's arrival, when applicable.

Baby's full name: _____

Date: _____

Time: _____

Weight: _____ **Length:** _____

Hair color: _____

Birthplace: _____

Length of labor: _____

Birth attendees: _____

The day's weather: _____

The day's headlines: _____

How, where, and when I learned of the birth: _____

_____

Looking Within

Spending time with your new grandchild can elicit abundant emotions that often rise to the surface once you're alone. Circle thoughts and feelings that you've experienced upon leaving your grandbaby.

Confidence	Hope
Contemplation	Insecurity
Contentment	Joy
Emptiness	Longing
Excitement	Lost in thought
Fatigue	Relief
Fulfillment	Sadness
Gratitude	Satisfaction
Helpfulness	Worry

Exploring Your Wisdom

What have you learned from your child's parenting style? How does your child's parenting affect you?

"Kids are hard—they drive you crazy and break your heart—whereas grandchildren make you feel great about life, and yourself, and your ability to love someone unconditionally, finally, after all these years." – Anne Lamott

Looking Within

Consider your parenting skills as a new mother. Who best assisted, advised, and supported you then? How can you do the same for your grandchild's parents?

Doing Your Part

What tasks and activities do you most enjoy doing for or with your grandchild? How does the baby express their feelings about each item you listed?

CAPTURE THE DETAILS!

My First Photo of My First Grandchild

TAPE PHOTO HERE!

Forming a Bond

Your sense of smell triggers memories like no other sense. Which aromas elicit thoughts of your mother? Which recall your own grandmother? Write down a few scents you would like to be known by.

Living in Love

Choosing your grandma name requires consideration, yet what you call your grandchild often flows without thought. What nicknames or terms of endearment have emerged as your favored monikers for the munchkin?

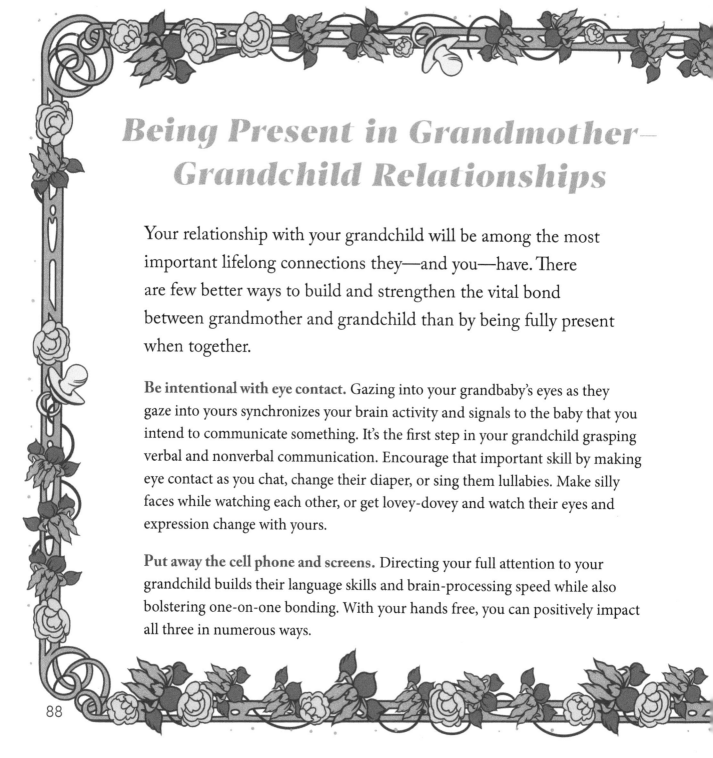

Being Present in Grandmother–Grandchild Relationships

Your relationship with your grandchild will be among the most important lifelong connections they—and you—have. There are few better ways to build and strengthen the vital bond between grandmother and grandchild than by being fully present when together.

Be intentional with eye contact. Gazing into your grandbaby's eyes as they gaze into yours synchronizes your brain activity and signals to the baby that you intend to communicate something. It's the first step in your grandchild grasping verbal and nonverbal communication. Encourage that important skill by making eye contact as you chat, change their diaper, or sing them lullabies. Make silly faces while watching each other, or get lovey-dovey and watch their eyes and expression change with yours.

Put away the cell phone and screens. Directing your full attention to your grandchild builds their language skills and brain-processing speed while also bolstering one-on-one bonding. With your hands free, you can positively impact all three in numerous ways.

Point out features of the baby's head and limbs to help them learn body parts. Doing the same in front of a mirror develops their sense of self. Introduce your grandchild to shapes, colors, textures, and sounds in their surroundings.

Recognize and empathize when powerful emotions emerge. Empathizing with your grandchild makes them feel understood and supported, leading to self-acceptance and understanding others. When your grandbaby seems upset for reasons unrelated to physical needs, try to get them to focus on your face and eyes. Copy their facial expressions and then change to calm ones, encouraging them to move beyond distress with you. When your toddler grandchild launches into rants or crying, tell them you know they're feeling something big and you want to understand it. Validating their feelings without judgment or fixing things helps them develop coping strategies.

Respond—instead of reacting—in tough situations. Your grandchild, and the situations and people connected to them, will inevitably test your patience. Rather than react with potentially damaging emotions or actions, take a breath or step away and consider reasons for your reaction. Then thoughtfully and calmly respond to the trigger. For example, when your grandchild won't stop crying no matter what you do, don't react with anger because you feel inadequate. Step away physically or figuratively, breathe deeply, consider reasons for your emotional reaction, and then let go of that and move toward calming the situation with a measured response.

Doing Your Part

Fill in the blanks of what you hope and wish for you and your grandchild together as they grow.

My grandchild loves my _____.

My grandchild _____

    when I _____.

My grandchild enjoys _____ with me.

My grandchild makes my _____.

"Every grandma has talents, education, and wisdom to share. These traits add up to power. You have the power to make a difference." – Harriet Hodgson

Looking Ahead

Use drawings, photos, and other pictures to create a colorful collage of a destination to which you long to introduce your grandchild.

Exploring Your Wisdom

Describe times your grandchild challenges the new parent in ways reminiscent of when that parent similarly challenged you. How did you feel as a mother? What's your perspective now?

"*Children are the rainbow of life. Grandchildren are the pot of gold.*"
– Irish blessing

Living in Love

When you coo about your grandchild to others, what is one thing you always say?

"A grandmother thinks of her grandchildren day and night, even when they are not with her. She will always love them more than anyone would understand."
– Karen Gibbs

Looking Ahead

What three challenges do you see for yourself in the future as a grandmother? For each, also include one thing that may ease your difficulty in that area.

1. _____

_____

_____

2. _____

_____

_____

3. _____

_____

_____

Forming a Bond

How has your shared love for your grandchild brought you and your child closer? In what ways has it impacted your relationship with your grandchild's other parent?

Being Present

Scribble time! Grab some crayons and scribble the feelings you're experiencing right now related to grandmotherhood. Let colors, scribble style, and intensity reflect the happenings in your head and heart.

"A grandmom's job is to sprinkle stardust into the lives of her grandchildren: to be a little bit parent, a little bit teacher, a whole lot best friend."
– Linda Oatman High

Living in Love

Grandmothers focus on ways their love can affect their grandchild's life. A fresh perspective: What are the specific ways that loving your grandchild has changed your life?

How to Become a Digital Grandma

Whether you're a long-distance grandma or if your grandchild lives around the corner, technology provides effective and inexpensive ways to connect with your favorite kiddo. From members-only sites for sharing family news and photos to multimedia messages highlighting your dear one's doings, digital services can ensure that you remain relevant to your grandchild despite any distance.

One way to minimize miles apart—or touch base across town—is with video chat apps such as FaceTime and Zoom. As children have brief attention spans and can't chat, these tips encourage bond-strengthening sessions where they need not utter a word.

- Chat with Mom or Dad as they hold, play with, or feed your grandchild so they regularly hear your voice.

- Arrange prenap chats to sing lullabies or read brief stories.

- Once your grandchild can be minimally attentive, read short picture books to them.

- Hold the baby's attention with toys you shake, rattle, and reveal.

- Be on standby for quick calls when meltdowns require a Grandma distraction.

- Kids + pets = success. Turn the camera around and let your grandchild see your animals.

- Use app options for screen sharing to play attention-grabbing videos for your grandchild.

- Provide guided tours of Grandma's house between visits. Holiday season tours can be especially engaging.

- When all else fails, peekaboo continues to be a crowd-pleaser.

- Last but not least: Don't take offense when your grandchild seems uninterested. Be assured it's not you—attention spans are short, and focusing on screens takes practice.

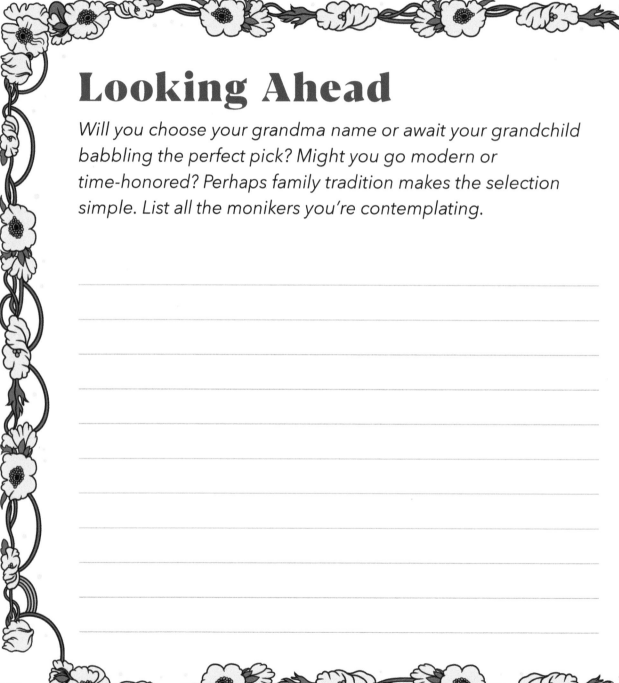

Looking Ahead

Will you choose your grandma name or await your grandchild babbling the perfect pick? Might you go modern or time-honored? Perhaps family tradition makes the selection simple. List all the monikers you're contemplating.

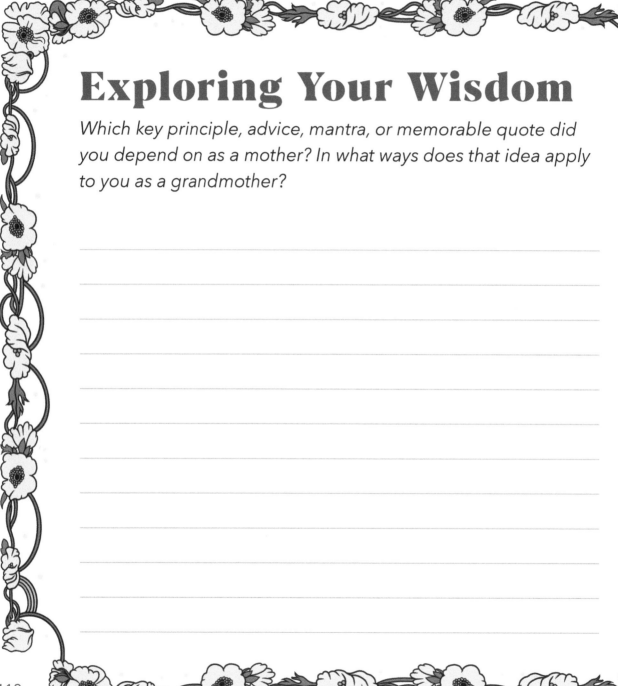

Exploring Your Wisdom

Which key principle, advice, mantra, or memorable quote did you depend on as a mother? In what ways does that idea apply to you as a grandmother?

"*You make all your mistakes with your own children so by the time your grandchildren arrive, you know how to get it right.*" – Liz Fenton

Looking Ahead

What stories of when your child was young will you share with your grandchild?

Being Present

What have you learned by viewing the world through your grandchild's eyes?

"Grandparents have a serious responsibility to hug and to snuggle, to play what the child wants to play, and to help the spirit flourish." – Jane Isay

Looking Within

How does your pre-grandbaby vision of what it would be like to be a grandmother compare with the reality of being one?

_____

_____

_____

_____

_____

_____

_____

_____

_____

_____

_____

_____

_____

_____

"Being a good grandma or grandpa is surprisingly easy. All you have to do is show up." – Marianne Waggoner Day

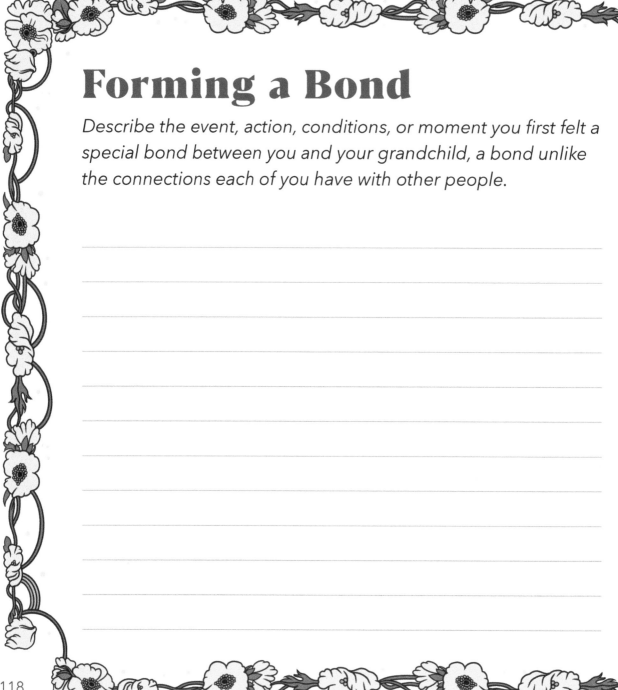

Forming a Bond

Describe the event, action, conditions, or moment you first felt a special bond between you and your grandchild, a bond unlike the connections each of you have with other people.

Looking Within

What historic events or cultural norms contributed to shaping your parenting style? How do those factors affect the way you approach being a grandmother?

Looking Ahead

What current attitudes and practices in our society do you foresee creating complicated situations for your grandchild's parents as they raise their child? What advice would you offer?

_____

_____

_____

_____

_____

_____

_____

_____

_____

_____

_____

_____

_____

_____

"Having a grandmother is like having an army. This is a grandchild's ultimate privilege: knowing that someone is on your side, always, whatever the details."
— Fredrik Backman

Exploring Your Wisdom

The pages of this journal feature several heartfelt quotes on grandmotherhood. Time to write your own quote-worthy tidbit. Use the starter phrase or go free form.

"Being a grandmother _____."

_____

_____

_____

_____

_____

_____

_____

_____

_____

_____

What Does Spoiling Your Grandchild Look Like?

Grandmothers spoil grandchildren, though spoiling specifics vary. In the space below, depict examples of your spoiling style, from scenes of special moments together to lists of goodies you shower upon your grandchild. Doodle or draw, write a list or poem, or create a collage to fill the space as suits your style.

Doing Your Part

Which lullabies do you sing to your grandchild? Are they traditional lullabies, popular songs, or made-up ditties? Do you sing the lullabies, or are you more apt to hum? Record your lullaby routine here.

Looking Within

What do you see of yourself in your grandchild? What feelings arose when you first realized that you could glimpse yourself in them?

"Of all of the life stages in later life, grandparenting stands out as the most positive."
– Lori K. Bitter

Forming a Bond

Love and attention matter most when creating bonds, yet material goods can strengthen them. Which heirloom items, personalized pieces, or similarly sentimental "stuff" will you give your grandchild? Why those?

Doing Your Part

What specific practices, rules, and guidelines set by your grandchild's parents will you adamantly support and enforce as your grandchild grows, especially when the child inevitably protests?

Being Present

List your top 10 must-remember moments, large or small, from your first 12 months as a grandmother.

1. _____

2. _____

3. _____

4. _____

5. _____

6. _____

7. _____

8. _____

9. _____

10. _____

CAPTURE THE DETAILS!

My First Grandchild's First Birthday

Date: _____ **Location:** _____

Guests in attendance: _____

My gift to my grandchild: _____

My grandchild's reaction to their birthday festivities: _____

_____

Photos of the fun:

TAPE PHOTOS AND
CAPTIONS HERE

Write a Letter

If you could travel back in time to when you first heard you were going to be a grandma, what would you tell yourself?

Oh, the places you've gone since first hearing, "You're going to be a grandma!" Consider the highs and lows, the ways you've grown, and the instances of "If only I'd known." Write a letter to yourself, heartfelt and true, with insight on the transformational journey from grandma-to-be to the grandma you are now.

Resources

Books, websites, and more pertaining to grandmotherhood, relationships, mindfulness, and engaging with your grandchild.

BOOKS

Grandparenting: Renew, Relive, Rejoice by Pam Siegel and Leslie Zinberg

Nanaville: Adventures in Grandparenting by Anna Quindlen

Real World Mindfulness for Beginners: Navigate Daily Life One Practice at a Time by Brenda Salgado

The Shared Wisdom of Mothers and Daughters: The Timelessness of Simple Truths by Alexandra Stoddard

Toad Cottages & Shooting Stars: Grandma's Bag of Tricks by Sharon Lovejoy

Unconditional Love: A Guide to Navigating the Joys and Challenges of Being a Grandparent Today by Jane Isay

ARTICLES

"How to Be a Good Mother-in-Law and Grandmother," VeryWellFamily.com/be-good-mother-in-law-grandmother-1695761

"How to Honor Boundaries as a Grandparent," VeryWellFamily.com
/grandparents-who-have-problems-with-boundaries-1695778

"Sharing the Caring: Partnering with Your Adult Child to Care for Your
Grandchild," ZerotoThree.org/resources/440-sharing-the-caring
-partnering-with-your-adult-child-to-care-for-your-grandchild

WEBSITES

GrandyCamp.info

GrandMagazine.com

HealthyChildren.org

LiveAbout.com

ReadBrightly.com

TinyBuddha.com

PODCASTS

The Grand Life: Grandparenting Our Grands: TheGrandLife.libsyn.com/

APPS

Infant.io—animations and puzzles that help stimulate a baby's mind

KidloLand—an educational app with nursery rhymes for babies and kids

Tinybeans—for storing your favorite family moments

Vroom—science-based tips for helping a baby's brain development

References

Backman, Fredrik. *My Grandmother Sends Her Regards and Apologises.* Hodder & Stoughton, 2016. Quoted on page 123.

Bitter, Lori K. *The Grandparent Economy: How Baby Boomers Are Bridging the Generation Gap.* Rochester, NY: Paramount Market Publishing, Inc., 2015. Quoted on page 129.

Day, Marianne Waggoner. *Camp Grandma: Next-Generation Grandparenting—Beyond Babysitting.* Berkeley, CA: She Writes Press, 2019. Quoted on page 117.

Girando, Jan Miller, and Mary Engelbreit. *When a Child Is Born, So Is a Grandmother.* Kansas City, MO: Andrews McMeel Publishing, 1999. Quoted on page 5.

Good, Honey. *Stories for My Grandchild: A Grandmother's Journal.* New York: Abrams Noterie, 2019. Quoted on page 4.

Greeley, Andrew M., and Mary G. Durkin *The Book of Love: A Treasury Inspired by the Greatest of Virtues.* New York: Tom Doherty Associates, 2008. Quoted on page 47.

High, Linda Oatman *The Hip Grandma's Handbook: Tips, Resources, and Inspiration for the New Breed of Grandmother.* New York: Falls Media, 2007. Quoted on page 103.

Hodgson, Harriet. *The Grandma Force: How Grandmothers, Changing Grandchildren, Families, and Themselves*. Omaha, NE: WriteLife Publishing, 2019. Quoted on page 91.

Isay, Jane. *Unconditional Love: A Guide to Navigating the Joys and Challenges of Being a Grandparent Today*. New York: Harper Collins, 2018. Quoted on page 115.

Kidd, Sue Monk, and Ann Kidd Taylor. *Traveling with Pomegranates: A Mother and Daughter Journey to the Sacred Places of Greece, Turkey, and France*. New York: Penguin Publishing Group, 2009. Quoted on page 33.

Lamott, Anne, and Sam Lamott. *Some Assembly Required: A Journal of My Son's First Son*. New York: Penguin Publishing Group, 2013. Quoted on page 79.

Middenway, Rob, and Karen Gibbs. *A Gallery of Scrapbook Creations: Great Scrapbook Designs to Inspire You*. Quoted on page 97.

Mirror.co.uk. "I'm a Grandad Now but I Still Don't Feel Grown-Up: Kevin Whately on His Life without Morse." March 2, 2007. mirror.co.uk/news/uk-news/im-a-grandad-now-but-i-still-dont-455737. Quoted on page 41.

Newmark, Amy. *Chicken Soup for the Soul: Grandparents: 101 Stories of Love, Laughs and Lessons across the Generations*. Cos Cob, CT: Chicken Soup for the Soul, 2019. Quoted on pages 13 and 95.

Paston, Bryna Nelson. *How to Be the Perfect Grandma*. Naperville, IL: Sourcebooks, Inc., 2002. Quoted on page 53.

Stahl, Lesley. *Becoming Grandma: The Joys and Science of the New Grandparenting*. New York: Blue Rider Press, 2016. Quoted on page 61.

Steinke, Lisa, and Liz Fenton. *The Year We Turned Forty: A Novel*. New York: Washington Square Press, 2016. Quoted on page 111.

Strachey, Ray. *A Quaker Grandmother, Hannah Whitall Smith*. Creative Media Partners, 2018. Quoted on page 27.

Witkovsky, Jerry. *The Grandest Love: Inspiring the Grandparent-Grandchild Connection*. Bloomington, IN: Xlibris US, 2013. Quoted on page 9.

Acknowledgments

Considering what to write here has been one of the more challenging tasks of the book for me. I owe deep thanks and gratitude to many dear ones; my fingers are crossed in hopes that I leave no one out.

First and foremost, I thank acquisitions editor, Vanessa Putt, for reaching out to me for this project. I never considered a journal as my first book; I sincerely appreciate that you did.

An equal amount of thanks and appreciation goes to my editor, Andrea Leptinsky, for your direction and your assuaging my newbie concerns with nary an eye roll (I hope).

To my grandson, Brayden, I could not have written about being a first-time grandmother without you. You were my first grandchild. Because of you, I know much of what being a first-time grandmother is about. Thank you.

To the six grandchildren—six *grandsons*—who came after Brayden: Camden, Declan, James, Tyler, Benjamin, and one not yet born as I write this (though I do know you're a boy). Thank you for teaching me again and again how big one grandma's heart—and patience—can grow.

To my extraordinary daughters and their exceptional husbands—Brianna and Patrick, Megan and Preston, Andrea and Allen. I'm endlessly grateful to you for creating and sharing those most grand of grandsons. Thank you, too, for the show of support in all I do and your adherence to my "do not disturb" demands despite stories you wanted to share and surprises you wished to shower upon me.

My deepest thanks to my husband, Jim, the PawDad and PawPaw to my Gramma. You found the right balance. You supported me yet stayed away (or silent) in ways I needed most. You are my rock.

And to all the grandmothers I've met along my grandmother journey who shared their stories and their hearts, those I've known for decades, and those I've never met in person yet consider my friends, thank you for the edification and the examples you've set. I'm a better grandmother because of you.

Lastly, to Becky, my older sister, dear friend, and fellow grandma, your passing will forever be part of the story of writing my first book. You loved hard and hugged long—and the other way around, too. Your laugh and your light live on in my heart.

About the Author

 Lisa Carpenter is a blogger and freelance writer. She founded GrandmasBriefs.com in 2009 soon after her first grandson's first birthday. On the blog, Lisa highlights the vitality and relevance of today's grandmothers and shares the good, bad, humorous, helpful, and heartwarming of her grandmother lifestyle.

Lisa's freelance writing credits include *Woman's World*, The Huffington Post, Considerable.com, Purple Clover, and many others.

Lisa and her husband of nearly four decades have three daughters, three sons-in-law, and seven grandsons. They live in Colorado with one senior cat and an American Bully rescue dog who shamelessly slobbers all over the grandkids when they visit.

CPSIA information can be obtained
at www.ICGtesting.com
Printed in the USA
LVHW051103220522
718846LV00001B/1

9 781647 398859